The Way Back,

The Six Virtues

by Mark Zaretti

© 2019 The Way Back Group Ltd. All Rights Reserved.

https://thewaybackmeditation.org

ISBN 978-1711080598

Books in The Way Back series
by Mark Zaretti:

Book 1. Guidance for the Seeker of TRUTH
Second Edition

Book 2. The Way Back, The Six Virtues

Coming soon:

Book 3. The Way Back to TRUTH

Book 4. The Way Back, Book of GRACE

Table of Contents

Preface 1
Part 1: Origins of The Way Back 2
    Chapter 1: Meditation Teacher Mark 2
    Chapter 2: Attaining Enlightenment 2
    Chapter 3: Moving Abroad 3
    Chapter 4: First Contact 4
    Chapter 5: Back in the UK 5
    Chapter 6: Writing Begins 5
    Chapter 7: The Channelled Book 6
    Chapter 8: Establishing The Way Back 6
Part 2: Soul and Spirit 7
    Chapter 1: Your Soul 8
    Chapter 2: Soul Journey 9
    Chapter 3: Karma 10
    Chapter 4: Your Spirit 11
    Chapter 5: Both Soul and Spirit Matter 13
Part 3: Ego 14
Part 4: The Six Virtues 16
    Chapter 1: The Six Virtues Lead to Harmony 22
    Chapter 2: Applying the Six Virtues 24
    Chapter 3: The Importance of Trust 27
Part 5: Living the Six Virtues 29
    Chapter 1: Humility 30
    Chapter 2: Gratitude 31
    Chapter 3: Non-judgment 32
    Chapter 4: Respect 33
    Chapter 5: Compassion 33
    Chapter 6: Unconditional love 39
Part 6: Putting it into Practice 41
    Chapter 1: Principles 43
    Chapter 2: Practice 46
    Chapter 3: Ethos 48
Postface 50

Preface

This book is a follow-up to *"Guidance for the Seeker of TRUTH"* which was first published in December 2016 but you do not need to have read that book in order to learn about and benefit from *"The Six Virtues"* right now. This book stands on its own and has been intentionally written so that it makes sense even if you are completely new to the subject of spirituality, meditation and things like souls and karma.

The core knowledge shared within this book is based on information channelled while writing *"The Way Back to TRUTH"*, which is not scheduled to be published for a few years. However I truly believe that The Six Virtues are so powerful and transformative that I want you to have this opportunity to learn about them and start benefiting by incorporating them into your life right away.

This book provides guidance on The Six Virtues that is not found within the other books and so without further ado I present to you *"The Way Back: The Six Virtues"* written with love and kindness.

Your humble guide,
Mark P Zaretti.

Part 1: Origins of The Way Back
Chapter 1: Meditation Teacher Mark

Mark, the first of three triplets to arrive was born in 1974 in the south east of England and like many young children he was naturally psychic. By the age of seven he had intuitively discovered basic breath meditation, crystal and aura awareness and was interested in the more spiritual side of life.

While studying biology at the University of Manchester in the 90's he came across energy based light and sound meditation and not long after started teaching alongside and learning from more experienced teachers.

After 13 months of intensive mantra and breath meditation practice where he sat for two or more hours every day and up to six hours in one sitting each weekend he was given access to light and sound energy.

He began to explore energies and levels of consciousness that went far beyond the realms of mind, astral body, kundalini or anything he had experienced up to that point, and he knew he had discovered something special.

Chapter 2: Attaining Enlightenment

Fast forward 12 years and about 8,000 hours of meditation later and Mark attained enlightenment in the first few days of a ten day meditation. During those years he helped teach and mentor many meditators in Kent and the north of England running regular classes and weekend workshops.

For him spirituality was never about a belief system or dogma, it had always been about direct spiritual experience and the realisations they provide. He increasingly found though that the groups he had studied with and worked alongside on his own journey were getting increasingly embroiled in politics and personalities and were losing sight of the big picture. They were forgetting that it was all about love and importantly sharing the gift with others. He chose to carry on helping people by teaching independently of any particular system or group.

Chapter 3:   Moving Abroad

In December of 2014 Mark rented out his house in Leeds, packed his camper van and took Blue his collie dog to Italy so he could improve his Italian and distance himself further from the negativity he was experiencing in the north of England.

He spent about 15 months in Italy living first on Lake Como before relocating east of Rome in a quiet village alongside vineyards. However it was just before leaving the lake that he got a call from an old friend he knew from a meditation group in Manchester. This call would eventually change everything, and looking back it was obvious that the universe made sure that call happened.

Because of that phone call Mark became aware of something he had heard about years before but had never pursued; that there were enlightened spiritual teachers who had *"ascended"* upon their death and now watched over and guided humanity from higher spiritual realms.

These *"ascended masters"* as they were known were working directly with the two enlightened teachers who had first revealed the light and sound energy to Mark and this meant that more people were being given the ability to pass on this amazing energy.

Chapter 4:   First Contact

These were exciting times and while still in Italy Mark reached out to the ascended masters and made contact via a psychic process known as clairaudience, which allowed him to tune in and communicate with them directly, obviously with a lot of practice.

Little did he know that he was being guided by them and it was all part of a much bigger plan, one that required him to return to the UK. Sure enough he got a call a few weeks later from his friend Johnathan who owned the holiday apartment he was staying in explaining he would have to vacate in a few weeks as they had taken an out of season booking. It was time to leave Italy and Mark headed back to the UK, eventually returning to Kent.

Chapter 5:   Back in the UK

Within a few weeks of returning he found himself teaching meditation, first to one or two people, but soon the groups got larger and in time he was running weekly classes with up to 60 people attending. It seemed he was where he was meant to be.

Chapter 6:   Writing Begins

Rewinding the story a little though, when Mark first returned to Kent there was an important task that he was asked to do by the Spiritual Hierarchy. If you are not familiar with the phrase *"Spiritual Hierarchy"* it is the collective name often used to refer to the ascended masters and other spiritual beings guiding humanity from higher dimensions.

The Spiritual Hierarchy asked Mark to write an article about the importance of grace, humility and love on the spiritual journey. This article was the start of Mark beginning the role that the Spiritual Hierarchy had planned for him, he was to be their scribe. That evening he sat for many hours in deep focus and channelled the article, spending time over the following days to check and cross check every sentence for accuracy and truth.

He worked closely with Portia who was another enlightened teacher and a powerful psychic and on the 6th of September 2016 that first article was published as a blog on Mark's meditation website with the title *"The Role of Grace, Humility and Love on a Meditation Journey to Enlightenment"*.

Chapter 7: The Channelled Book

Now that he had proven he was ready and able to carry out the work they intended the Spiritual Hierarchy set him the task of writing the book. This book was intended to guide the many new teachers and students around the world because many hundreds of people were now receiving light and sound initiation and they needed tangible and practical support.

That book was clairaudiently channelled over a 30 day period and was published in December of 2016 with the title *"Guidance for the Seeker of TRUTH"*.

Chapter 8: Establishing The Way Back

This almost brings you up to date and to the book you are holding right now but there was another task that the Spiritual Hierarchy asked Mark to do. Early in 2018 they asked Mark and Portia to formerly establish a school of meditation and to gather and train a small but focused group of meditators and teachers.

The names of those who were to be involved in this initial group were given to them by the Spiritual Hierarchy and included some who were already being taught by Mark and Portia as well as teachers from other countries.

The Spiritual Hierarchy were very specific about the name of this school, it was to be called *"The Way Back"* and the purpose of this group was not only to continue to provide and support initiations into spiritual light and sound meditation but importantly to teach and inspire those meditators how to bring their spiritual awareness and realisations back down into everyday life.

At the core of these teachings are *"The Six Virtues"* and the purpose of the book you now hold in your hands is to share with you an overview of this guidance on how to better integrate as a spiritual person and get the most out of your journey and indeed life too, if you wish.

Part 2: Soul and Spirit

Most people have heard about the idea of soul or spirit and if you have read *"Guidance for the Seeker of TRUTH"* or *"The Way Back to*

TRUTH" then you will know that they do indeed exist and are a very special part of you. But if you have not yet read those books do not worry, this book is independent of them and you will learn things here that you wont find there.

Just be sure to avoid the confusion that some people have when they mix the soul and spirit up, since these are two completely different things as will be explained.

Both your soul and spirit rest within you at the core of your body and when life is looked at from a higher perspective they really are the reason why you are here now. The *"here now"* referred to is of course the 3rd dimension, what most people know as Earth, the physical world and so on.

But its not too important at this time to understand the finer details of what a soul is or what a spirit is and how they came to be, that is explored in great detail in *"The Way Back to TRUTH"*.

Chapter 1: Your Soul

What is useful to understand at this time is that your soul is your enduring personality which has little to do with this body you find yourself within. Your soul existed well before you were born and it will still be around a long time after you have let go of your last breath. Your soul endures and this body you have is an amazing vehicle allowing your soul to experience the world around you.

Chapter 2: Soul Journey

You see your soul is on a journey and each body you have is a different vehicle, allowing it to progress a bit further along that journey. All journeys have a destination and your soul is aiming to get back to the highest form of love, or more precisely your soul is trying to embrace and express the highest form of love, that which is unconditional.

But like many journeys into new territory your soul does not get there in a straight line, much like a child playing the game of *"warmer or colder"* where the child seeks a hidden reward like a sweet and as the child moves around the room the person who hid it says *"warmer"* if the child moves towards it or *"colder"* if the child moves further away. Eventually, with enough guidance, the child finds the sweet and their journey is rewarded.

Well your soul is looking for the highest kind of love and down here on the 3rd dimension is where the game is played. Only instead of someone saying *"warmer"* or *"colder"* spiritual guides, your intuition and even your conscience are guiding you towards it. Of course if you are moving in the wrong direction it helps to know and the universe has that covered too. This is where karma comes into play.

Chapter 3:   Karma

Karma is not there to punish you as many people misunderstand, it is simply feedback, letting you know that you have gone in the wrong direction and moved away from love. If you move very far from love in your choices and actions, for example getting angry, hateful, judgmental and so forth, then you have probably generated bad feelings and thoughts and things will be getting pretty negative in life.

When you get negative you create your own karma which acts to redress the imbalance and let you know something is not right. Because you are moving in the wrong direction then karma will also provide life-lessons to help you learn from your mistakes.

If you do not learn the lesson that karma has provided then you are carrying on in the wrong direction making even more negativity and so the lessons will continue to repeat getting stronger until your karma manifests in big ways in your life, which can include health issues, accidents or general friction and problems.

So with higher guidance helping you and karma also giving you feedback your soul has many lifetimes to get as close to expressing higher love as possible.

The metaphoric candy is not forgotten either because if you get close enough in this life (or a future one) then the rewards can be amazing. Have you ever wondered why some people are naturally drawn towards the wonders of higher meditation with some attaining *"enlightenment"*? Beyond even that imagine living for millions of years on higher dimensions as a highly evolved spiritual being made of energy, light and love, free of your physical body and you start to get an idea.

So if you are thinking *"that sounds great, how do I move in the right direction?"* then one of the most important keys is The Six Virtues. Of course being wise you will also realise that it is not about chasing the end of the journey it is about loving, living and learning from every step of that journey.

Chapter 4: Your Spirit

But before we introduce these Six Virtues that are the key to this journey it is worth remembering that you also have a spirit within you. Spirit is very pure and so does not have much sense of personality. In fact your spirit is so pure that it can contain the highest love possible without contaminating it. This love is that which is greater than anything you can experience in everyday life, even in the deepest of relationships.

Just like your soul your spirit is also on a journey but what it is seeking is to find the origin of that highest love, that which is pure, beyond creation, what some call *"The Source"*, *"Enlightenment"*, *"God"*, *"Unity"* and so on, so that it can become filled with this highest love and radiate it out into the world.

These are just words and wise people know that a words like these are an attempt to describe something that is pretty much indescribable in the same way that words can do a good job of giving an idea of something but they never replace the actual experience of it. If you want to know what it is like to ride a horse then you will have to get on a horse.

So whereas the soul journey is one of becoming more loving the journey of the spirit is to return to the source of love. Your soul requires the world around it in order to have experiences from which it can learn about love and as such the soul journey is worked on in every day life. By contrast the spirit wants to let go of all the distractions of the world around you so that it can find that ultimate stillness and peace behind everything which created love and as such the spiritual journey is worked on predominantly in meditation.

Although the methods of travel vary both your soul and your spirit are on a journey trying find **the way back** to love. Both journeys are of equal importance and you cannot truly find the way back if you focus on just the spirit or just the soul.

Chapter 5: Both Soul and Spirit Matter

If the spiritual journey is likened to a thirsty person in the desert looking for a water well, then your soul journey would be likened to making sure you have first created a bucket suitable to retrieve and carry the precious water you desire within it. Otherwise you shall get to the well but have no means to explore its depths and bring back the water that you could then enjoy and be sustained by.

The way back requires the conscious development of the soul and if the opportunity arises then the embracing of the spiritual journey. The soul is the limiting factor in your spiritual journey because if the soul is not ready then even if you have the opportunity to try advanced forms of meditation your practice will be fruitless and progress will be difficult.

If the soul is not developed then even enlightenment will be unfulfilling because you cannot have one exalted without the other. The key to you discovering the way back and thus harmoniously integrating the spiritual and soul journeys is the The Six Virtues.

Part 3:   Ego

The word *"ego"* just like the words *"karma"*, *"soul"* and *"spirit"* is one of those words that most people have an awareness of, but seldom have the opportunity to understand fully. Ego is an actual thing, just like your soul and your spirit. But unlike your soul and spirit ego does not come from higher energies and realms and does not have a desire towards a greater love.

Ego is the opposite of your spirit and it plays a tug of war with you pulling you down into the physical world of desire and division. The spirit as you now understand is trying to take you out of desire and back to oneness, the opposite of division, to make you truly whole and complete.

In any given moment you have a choice, it may be trivial like choosing to stop and give directions to a stranger who is clearly lost, or pretending you are too busy and walking on by without making eye contact. It could be a great decision like choosing not to get involved in a criminal activity and just saying no to peer pressure or giving in and talking your first steps down a path of wrongdoing.

The examples are endless but when you look closely you will see that the choice you have is fundamentally always the same. Do you listen to your heart, soul and conscience and do what you know deep down is *"good"* or do you do what you know deep down is *"wrong"*.

With every single choice you make, big or small, you are either moving more towards love or more away from it. It is this duality that allows you to learn from these choices and whenever you move away from love you build up karma. Ego is not itself bad, it simply reinforces your desires which come from your personality.

So when you are motivated too much by what you want then you become selfish and your ego takes over. When you live more from your heart and soul then you become more selfless and your soul takes over.

It is really that simple in principle but in practice you live in the most dualistic and desire driven environment that exists and every single person has some ego. Ego holds you back in relationships, in life, in meditation and on both your soul and spiritual journeys and for this reason the Spiritual Hierarchy channelled The Six Virtues, to help free you from your ego.

Part 4: The Six Virtues

When people first hear words like *"spiritual guides"*, *"ascended masters"* or *"a spiritual hierarchy"*, some get caught up on the words because they suggest that your own journey may have a dependency on others and your ego wants to believe that your are fully in control of everything.

But on all dimensions there are exchanges of energy, just as a plant is dependant on the sun for light so too your spiritual journey is dependant on the source for spiritual light and so on.

There are different levels and different vibrations throughout duality and within higher dimensions there are spiritual beings with correspondingly different roles. This concept may help you understand the structure of the universe, spiritual dimensions and ultimately creation.

For example spiritual guides are on a higher vibration than you which provides the basis of your trust towards them. This trust is born of the understanding that spiritual guides, being of a higher positive vibration are potentially closer to love and also have a higher perspective. Above them are the ascended masters and above them are higher beings.

Above all is the source of unconditional love, which is Unity, which is God.

But it is important to also understand that unconditional love is the energy which not only manifests but also pervades every dimension, including where you are now. So in this way you and spiritual guides are also connected by love and are part of a larger whole, of unconditional love.

When you progress on your spiritual journey, which can involve a process called *"initiation"*, then the vibrational awareness your spirit can have within meditation may go beyond the realms where spiritual guides reside, and yet spiritual guides can and will still guide you in meditation and are there to support your soul journey too.

It can get confusing, especially as you try to understand how spiritual guides interact with other spiritual beings, and that is even before you try and fathom the relationship between your soul, spirit and other parts of you like your mind, aura, ego and body. There are different parts of you and there are many different beings on different levels all making up this amazing creation.

Each part has its role and each part has its vibration. The nature of your human mind may lead you to naturally ask, *"which part is more important?"* or *"how do I relate to them?"*. Imagine an orchestra with different instruments. The cello makes a very low vibration compared to the violin. The kettle drum is deeper than the triangle. String and wind instruments can hold a note whereas percussion instruments create a beat. Thus each instrument has its own defined role. Which is more important? They are all important!

It is impossible to make harmonious music without all the instruments playing together in a coordinated way. Some stop to allow others to be heard, some harmonise, and some create contrast, but they are all needed.

Following the orchestra analogy, each musician understands their part, whether they understand the full picture or not. If one musician is out of sync then the music does not flow. With the idea of harmony in mind you are asked to really contemplate and reflect on these following virtues:

Humility

Gratitude

Respect

Non-judgement

Compassion

Unconditional Love

These Six Virtues help you to become more able to meditate; to channel love, healing and light; to be sensitive to the guidance from the Spiritual Hierarchy; and perhaps most tangibly to transform your life into one of harmonious joy living in alignment with love. It is always your choice.

But as a human having someone say to you "*be more humble*" or "*show unconditional love*" can feel like being talked down to, or being controlled, and this can have a negative outcome on the human condition.

Being told to "*foster gratitude*" can be translated by the ego as "*you are not grateful enough*". Whether it is true or not, your personality may feel worse as a result and although feelings are not the highest vibration you can experience, they are important because negative feelings hold you back.

Understand that the friction that may cause you to feel negative when reflecting on these virtues is caused by your ego and not your soul though. Your soul rejoices in these virtues because it is of a higher vibration, but your ego resists these virtues because these virtues weaken it.

Ego is after all, the opposite of unconditional love, and understanding this profoundly simple truth helps you realise the importance of these virtues. They help you overcome your ego so your true self can shine through.

These virtues are also how the highest of the spiritual beings on higher dimensions relate with each other. There is no *"looking up to"*, *"answering to"*, *"lording over"*, or *"being in awe of"* other beings. It is simply that those spiritual beings most aligned with love aspire to unconditional love for every other being.

Each aspires to show respect for every other being. Each spiritual being aspires to be humble before every other being. Each spiritual being aspires to be non-judgemental towards every other being. Each spiritual being fosters gratitude for every other being. Each spiritual being has compassion for every other being.

These Six Virtues describe not just the way the highest of the spiritual beings interact with each other but also how they interact with you. All beings and indeed all things ultimately came from unconditional love and on the higher dimensions they are closer to and more aware of this higher love and so have the potential to demonstrate it, whether they are light or spiritual beings or the spiritual guides and ascended masters who were once people just like you who lived in the physical world.

Chapter 1: The Six Virtues Lead to Harmony

Imagine that there is no ego, no emotions, and no agenda other than to honour and demonstrate love. The orchestra works together out of love, not out of fear, competition or ego. But what of these positive and loving individual beings on higher dimensions?

Each can aspire to have humility about itself. Each can aspire to have gratitude for itself. Each can aspire to have respect for itself. Each can aspire to be non-judgemental towards itself. Each can aspire to have compassion from itself. Each can aspire to have unconditional love for itself.

Each is a part of the whole and how they are towards other parts is ideally how they are towards themselves because they know they are part of a whole. When one is out of harmony they are all out of harmony.

Now consider what it is to be a human born into a world of duality and division down here on the 3rd dimension where everything seems very separate from everything else. You are not them, others are different from you. You can experience fear, mistrust, judgement, competition, and loss.

This illusion of separation can make you believe and feel like you are very much alone. Your mind, emotions and personality that create your ego can turn you inward into self-focus and you begin to build walls between you and others.

Now imagine a world where you "*know*" that separation is just an illusion. That how you act, think, feel and communicate affects everyone else as well as yourself. Imagine a world where everyone knows about higher things like spiritual guides and that they came from the unconditional love of the Source, God.

It is the natural consequence of the love behind everything that the universe desires for the world and every soul on it to make beautiful music, to be in harmony. Each of you comes from "*the source*" and is the result of unconditional love manifesting into creation.

You are not separate from higher dimensions and all within them, you are consciousness within the lower manifest dimensions. Just as different parts of creation are at different vibrations so too you are present at different vibrations but it is all an extension of duality which comes from the source, via grace, which is a very special thing indeed.

Those souls who act as spiritual guides for people alive at this time were once people just like you who walked on Earth within the illusion of separation, an illusion that was necessary for each of them to learn and raise their vibration more towards love, as you do now. Even on higher dimensions there is separation but there is much more clarity and understanding for those who seek it.

At the highest level everything is perfect and everything is as it is meant to be. Manifest creation and the world you live on are not a mistake and neither is your life; you and your life are the emanation of unconditional love into lower vibrational planes and there is a reason.

Chapter 2: Applying the Six Virtues

Separation is an illusion and with that understanding then it becomes clear that the virtues are not just to be applied at yourself. They are three fold in their application:

1. They apply to you.

2. They apply to what is around you. This includes your family and friends but it also includes every single person, animals and all life, the environment and the entire world.

3. They apply to that which came before you and is guiding you. Ultimately this means God but between you and God, the source, there are many higher beings within the Spiritual

Hierarchy including spiritual guides, angels, ascended masters and those above them.

When thinking of the Six Virtues and how to apply them it is not only powerful but also more transformative when you approach them from all three aspects of (1) self, (2) others and (3) above.

Sometimes it is easier to understand one of the virtues in relation to others, sometimes it is easier to do so in relation to yourself. But it is when you are able to demonstrate all the virtues in all three ways that you are truly transformed and uplifted.

The more you are humble about yourself; humble before fellow souls on Earth; and humble about your part within the overall big picture then the more you move with grace and your ego's hold on you is diminished. The same is true of the other virtues and qualities.

The more you are grateful of yourself, of others, and of those that watch over and care for you, the more you open up to the flow of love between all things finally connected to and aligned with love and your life's true purpose can unfold with ease.

The more you respect yourself, those around you, and that which is divine then the more you are able to positively influence your world and also be supported by it.

The more you are non-judgemental of yourself, of others, and of that which is above, then the more you have the space to allow yourself to discover the truth of things and ultimately to move towards the truth that *"we are one"*.

The more compassion you show from yourself, towards others and that which is above then the more compassion you will be surrounded by and receive.

The more you practice unconditional love towards yourself, towards others, and the source or God then the more you allow connectedness and love to manifest into your life and reach others too.

So you see that the desire for people to practice these virtues and qualities is not a mandate passed down to humans from on high, neither is it judgement, punishment or criticism. Rather it is guidance to help you live in tune with the natural order of the cosmos on all dimensions.

Disorder and suffering comes from letting the illusion of separation dictate an egocentric life which has fear at its core. These Six Virtues are not a burden to limit your life rather they are the key to set your soul and indeed your spirit free. They are the way all the parts within the greater whole naturally create harmonious music and a reminder to you that you can be part of this beautiful orchestra, which ultimately is conducted by unconditional love.

Chapter 3: The Importance of Trust

Although it is amazing for those who pursue the spiritual journey to ultimately realise the state of enlightenment, it is not the full picture. For those who are dedicated then the opportunity exists to fully integrate with their state, whether they are enlightened, initiated or yet to be. It is through practising the Six Virtues that you become more integrated at all stages of your personal journey.

Even if you are not meditating and going into higher realms gaining higher states of consciousness to integrate with, you still have your soul, spirit and heart to integrate with in everyday life. In other words there is the opportunity to integrate on every level, and great benefit from doing so too.

For this spiritually authentic integration to happen it is vital that all of the virtues are embraced, irrespective of whether you are meditating but one of the ways that people hold themselves back is by not trusting.

It is easy to accept things you can see and touch, but it takes trust to accept that which is not yet within your awareness. But you cannot say you are humble, grateful, respectful, non-judgemental, compassionate, or unconditionally loving of the guidance and support that the Spiritual Hierarchy including spiritual guides give and yet at the same time not trust in them or believe in their existence.

A lack of trust manifests as fear and doubt, both of which are negative. If for example you have asked for guidance and having received it you start to question the guidance and focus on obstacles and your own doubts, then you give energy to those obstacles and your doubts and are demonstrating that you do not trust that the universe can support you.

So a lack of trust is effectively rejecting help from above and understanding this is useful because it gives you a tangible way of recognising when you are drifting out of alignment from the virtues, in other words, if you find yourself doubting or finding it difficult to trust.

When people first learn about the virtues they initially grasp them intellectually and philosophically, but it takes a deeper desire, intention and will power to really start living them consciously within your core and to nurture them in your heart.

This is where trust, or lack of trust, can be a valuable indicator of where you are in your own spiritual adoption of the Six Virtues. If you find yourself struggling to trust higher guidance, or you are giving in to your own fears and doubts about change, then this feedback provides you a way of recognising that you may be out of alignment from your soul, guidance and from the virtues.

If this does happen simply stop, be kind to yourself and forgive yourself because fear and doubt are a natural aspect of the lower personality and come from ego. Have the intention to change direction, raising above your lower personality and ego and focus more into your heart, soul and higher love.

Once you spot any problem then you are empowered to do something about it. You can ask your spiritual guide to help you embrace the Six Virtues and to strengthen your trust. There is so much you can do within your meditation and also in everyday life to begin to live the virtues more fully and having a strong intention to be aware of the virtues and come from a place of love is a good start.

Part 5: Living the Six Virtues

Understanding that the virtues are actual qualities, energies and vibrations will help you to explore some of the ways that they can be further developed and worked upon in life so that you can become a more virtuous person, integrating the highest attributes of love into your very being.

Chapter 1: Humility

Humility is an energy which exists within the chambers of your heart. The energy of humility can be channelled into your heart to help you become more humble. You could sit with your eyes closed and with deep sincerity you could say *"I channel humility into my heart"*, or *"I channel humility to myself"*. Of course you are free to find your own words.

You can also ask your spiritual guide to help you become more humble, but again sincerity is the key. It is your responsibility to develop your humility, not theirs, but if you are sincerely trying then they can help you. You can also pray to be guided to become more humble and you will learn more about the spiritual nature of prayer in the next book *"The Way Back to TRUTH"*.

A lovely exercise to do is when you first wake up, before getting out of bed, just lay there and work on allowing yourself to feel humble so that it is not an intellectual exercise in thinking about humility but rather an exploration of the state of *"being humble"*.

Humility is intentionally listed as the first virtue with good reason. Without humility none of the other virtues can flourish within you. Humility is the bedrock upon which the other virtues stand firm. The importance of humility is because more so than any of the other virtues it diminishes your ego.

Although most people understand the meaning of *"humility"* it is altogether a different thing to be actively humble and it is certainly not the action of putting yourself down, far from it.

Mark was once asked *"how do you make yourself humble?"* to which he replied *"I imagine the other person to be very big and I make myself small, so that they become the bigger focus, in this way I do not make the mistake of putting myself before them in terms of importance"*. Of course this is just one way, and you can try it for yourself but also find your own way to develop humility.

Chapter 2: Gratitude

Gratitude is an energy which is located within your solar-plexus which is the chakra or energy centre midway between your navel and sternum. It is worth noting that the solar plexus is often referred to as the *"seat of the personality"* and how gratitude affects the personality and that the personality (ego) can either block or embrace gratitude.

As with humility gratitude can be channeled, you can ask your spiritual guide to help you develop gratitude and you can also sincerely pray to become more grateful.

A simple exercise is to lie in bed at night just before you sleep and think about all the simple things that you are grateful for in the day you just had. Try and find something about yourself, something about others and something about the bigger picture that you are grateful about.

Chapter 3: Non-judgment

Unlike humility and gratitude, non-judgement is not an energy, it is a quality of how you think. As such being non-judgemental is something you must learn. The default behaviour of any person is to judge, so learning to be non-judgemental is striving to break free from unconscious habits by becoming conscious in your thinking. When you practice being non-judgemental it becomes second-nature and you become a more virtuous person.

A simple exercise is to sit very still and allow your mind to become calm and then just observe whatever is in front of you. Every time you start to judge something or to try and label it, simply stop and become even stiller. From stillness just observe whatever is before you, accepting it for what it is without any judgment.

Chapter 4:   Respect

Respect is not an energy, it is an attitude of your mind and this means that developing respect can be approached as a way of choosing how you think. Since it is not an energy it cannot be channeled but you can still ask your spiritual guide for help and also pray sincerely to change.

Chapter 5:   Compassion

Most spiritually aware people will intuitively understand the vital need for compassion within human existence. More often it is noted for the ill effects of its absence. However it is only with a deeper understanding of what compassion is that it can increase within you and within humanity as a whole and so it shall be explored in more detail.

Compassion is not the by-product of being loving though the two often are seen as hand in hand. However compassion is its own thing, distinct from love, healing, will and other energies or qualities.

Compassion is a quality of your soul, meaning that your capacity for compassion is governed by the level of compassion in your soul. Every soul, and therefore every person, has at least a tiny amount of compassion and every person has the capacity for compassion, though it may be very underdeveloped in some.

When you observe a person who is suffering then the amount of compassion you have will trigger a simultaneous response both in terms of thoughts and also in terms of emotions. The more capacity for compassion you have the stronger the compassionate response in your mental and emotional bodies. This is not a conscious response and it cannot be premeditated. Your soul's compassion triggers your mental body to respond with *"empathy"* and at the same time your soul compassion triggers your emotional body to respond with *"sympathy"*. These two vibrations, mental empathy and emotional sympathy combine to create the *"energy of compassion"* which permeates your aura in the chest region and radiates outwards. If the person you have compassion for is within about 2 miles distance of where you are then they will actually receive this energy of compassion in their aura.

Their emotional body will be affected by your energy of compassion resulting in them *"feeling uplifted"* and hence the vibrational state of their emotional body becomes more positive. A more positive emotional body will have a positive influence on their mental body and they may detect this change, at least at an unconscious level. The result of your compassion is that the recipient is emotionally uplifted.

It would be natural to assume that the act of showing compassion has increased your capacity for compassion, or that the recipient automatically becomes more compassionate. However this is not the case. Compassion is the unconscious reaction of your mental body and emotions to the influence of your soul. Soul development however requires a conscious participation in the process, but since you cannot be deliberately compassionate then how do you become more compassionate?

When you are the recipient of compassion there are two things that can happen, you can be unconscious of it or you can be conscious of it. To help you understand this think of the following scenario. A child is riding their bicycle down a quiet rural street and falls off grazing their knee. In a nearby garden an elderly person sees the accident. The elderly person is not mobile enough to assist however being very compassionate they feel great empathy and sympathy for the fallen child.

In scenario (A) the child looks up and makes eye contact with the elderly person and in that moment the child recognises the compassion they are receiving.

In scenario (B) the child does not look up and so is unaware of the elderly observer or their compassion.

In both scenarios the energy of compassion reaches the child but it is only in scenario (A) that the child recognises that they are receiving compassion. In that moment of conscious recognition, the child's own capacity for compassion increases. You must receive compassion to grow in compassion; compassion is highly contagious. Having received compassion this child is more likely to demonstrate compassion towards others in the future.

But remember there must be some mental recognition by the recipient that they have received compassion, even if it is not intellectually voiced. Without their mental body being aware, then although the energy of compassion is received and the emotional vibration uplifted, there is no increase in compassion of the recipient.

Understanding all this leads to the understanding that you do not give compassion with the goal of increasing a person's compassion, you give compassion simply because you are compassionate.

The recipient of your compassion potentially benefits in two ways. Firstly, emotionally they feel uplifted, they feel loved and if they are consciously aware of the compassion then they feel more connected to others. It is easy to understand how this benefits humanity. Secondly if they are conscious of your compassion then their soul's level of compassion is increased and they will automatically become more compassionate towards others.

Since this is all outside of the conscious control of each of you then the process of humanity evolving towards more compassion is slow. But there is one way in which you can increase your compassion. It requires you to be spiritually awake to the fact that you are part of something much bigger.

As will be discussed in more detail in the book *"The Way Back to TRUTH"* you have a spiritual guide and that there are higher spiritual beings caring and watching over you. Prayer in its truest sense is not religious and when you pray with genuine compassion for the benefit of another person then these higher beings recognise your genuine compassion and raise your soul's level of compassion further.

It is important to emphasis that this is only *"when you pray with genuine compassion"* because without genuine compassion there is no prayer. True prayers for another person always contain compassion. Dogmatic praying within the limits of a religious faith is often done from guilt or a sense of duty or routine, and so often lacks sincerity and compassion and is therefore not a prayer. Lacking compassion they are not heard and your level of compassion remains unchanged.

Search deeply within yourself, be present in the moment and let your soul rather than ego guide your prayers and your prayers will be enriched with compassion.

Some may ask *"what if you pray for yourself?"*. Understand this, that you cannot have compassion for yourself, you can only experience sympathy for yourself.

Recall that the energy of compassion is formed when empathy (mental body) and sympathy (emotional body) combine. If you have only empathy for another then there is no compassion and you will be *"cold"* and emotionless in your response. You may be correct, you may be just but you will not help that person much.

If you have only sympathy for another or yourself, but lack empathy then your sympathy will become sorrow. Sorrow is a negative emotion and you will bring yourself and the other person down with your sorrow. There is only compassion when both sympathy and empathy combine.

Because you can only experience sympathy towards yourself and not empathy, then you will only ever experience sorrow when you dwell on a negative experience. This is why you cannot experience compassion for yourself because your mental body cannot empathise with itself.

You cannot increase your compassion for others through practice, desire, intention or asking your spiritual guide to help you grow in compassion. You can only increase your compassion through the action of genuine prayer. If you are lucky enough to receive compassion then you will become more compassionate. Now that you have this knowledge embrace prayer in its true meaning, and help compassion spread throughout humanity.

Chapter 6: Unconditional love

As well as residing within your heart chakra the energy of unconditional love also sits within the emotional part of your aura. Unconditional love is a much higher energy than the energy of the world around you and every day it is sent to humanity by higher spiritual beings.

This unconditional love enters you through the chakras on the top of your head and your capacity to receive unconditional love is determined by the amount of unconditional love you give out to others. The more unconditionally loving you are, the more capacity your aura has for unconditional love and the more will enter you filling your aura.

6.1   Unconditional Love Versus Love

The energy of "*love*" is not the same as the energy of "*unconditional love*". Love energy resides in the space around your heart whereas unconditional love is within your heart chakra and in your aura. Unconditional love is pure and perfect. Love as an energy is found within the lower and mid dimensions, but is not found in the higher dimensions. Unconditional love is found in all dimensions.

Consider that love is a more tangible form of unconditional love and although both are neutral love is at a lower vibration and for this reason it is experienced by people in life in the physical world. When you as a person feel love for another person it is usually love energy that you feel flowing between you. But when one of the highest spiritual beings loves you their love is unconditional. You can practice both but in terms of raising your vibration unconditional love is the higher goal.

It has been mentioned that you can channel energies, ask your guide for help and also pray to develop the Six Virtues. But these are not the only ways of developing the Six Virtues within you. You must find ways for yourself, because your soul development is not an intellectual process, it is about integrating the Six Virtues into the very core of your nature and so *"stop thinking and start doing"* is good advice.

Part 6: Putting it into Practice

For anyone wanting to live in a more spiritually harmonious way there is potentially great benefit to be had from receiving guidance and advice. Guidance means learning from others who have already experienced that which you aspire towards and can save you time and perhaps help you avoid making the mistakes they did when they began.

If you are already practicing then guidance, advice and teachings can help you avoid becoming stuck in a routine by challenging your habits and giving you an alternative perspective.

However living as a truly spiritual person should never be dogmatic or prescriptive, blindly following guidance or advice because spirituality is about your experiences and ultimately finding out the truth for yourself.

Any spiritual guidance, teaching or advice that is accepted without eventually being validated by your own experience is simply *"spiritual belief"* and although it can be inspiring and motivating, stopping at the level of belief alone falls well short of truly *"being spiritual"*.

With that understanding in mind then advice, guidance and teaching can be shared for the purpose of discovering the value within it without the ego of the teacher or the student getting in the way.

Mark would at times speak with people who talked of things like *"walking in the woods"*, *"listening to music"* or *"fishing"* as their *"meditation"*. Of course what they meant was that for them these were the most relaxing or contemplative experiences they had had, up till then.

He would gently challenge them on their understanding of what meditation was and sometimes people would say it was wrong of him to do so. However if he had not challenged their limiting beliefs or understanding of what meditation really could be then they would not have got past their own limits of experience.

Challenging their belief, for example that *"listening to music is meditative"*, did not mean that it devalued their experience of listening to music but rather it gave them the option to either stick with their limit or step beyond it. Challenging their belief gave them freedom of choice, rather than taking something away, their life was potentially enriched if they chose to make the next step and find out for themselves.

It is for this reason that when you or anyone is moving out of a routine or *"comfort zone"* in order to learn and evolve, it helps to provide guidance about how best to practice and prepare to progress. Guidance or advice is meant to produce change and any change will have to overcome inertia and since any change means something new, then giving clear guidance based on real experience helps set and manage expectations and orients the person towards a more successful outcome.

But following advice or guidance is ideally seen as *"practice"* and should never be done only *"because I was told to do it"*, but rather because *"I understood the value in doing it"*. The former is asleep, the latter is awake.

With that in mind here are guidelines that Mark teaches students on The Way Back, and you are invited to incorporate what you find useful and what resonates with where you are in your own spiritual evolution, within your own life at this time. What has the most value is what you find works for you.

Chapter 1: Principles

There is great value in understanding beliefs and principles, but there is greater value in transcending them by experiencing for yourself the truth that they allude to. All of these principles can and have been fully realised already by many who have followed the teachings and guidance of The Way Back:

1. The Way Back recognises the existence of the human soul and human spirit as distinct aspects of a human being. Aura, meridian, chakras, mind, emotional body, etheric and other subtle vehicles also make up the human experience.

2. The Way Back recognises that the soul is on a journey over many lifetimes to raise its vibration towards love. The soul and thus the core of the personality survives death.

3. The Way Back recognises that a spirit may undertake the spiritual journey to enlightenment through meditation on spiritual light and sound energy, under the guidance of a living enlightened master. The nature of spirit is eternal.

4. The Way Back recognises that at times there is a spiritual master on the planet who can reveal spiritual light and sound energy and ultimately progress those ready towards enlightenment.

5. The Way Back recognises that humanity is guided by the higher spiritual beings, spiritual guides, and ascended masters of the

Spiritual Hierarchy, who serve God and have unconditional love as their guiding principle.

6. The Way Back recognises that there are dimensions higher than the 3rd dimension within which mankind is normally aware. All dimensions are created by God and humanity can explore these higher dimensions via spiritual light and sound meditation when a spiritual master is present on the planet.

7. The Way Back recognises that through meditation, prayer and inner stillness a person can receive guidance directly from their spiritual guide on matters of life, the soul and spiritual journeys.

8. The Way Back has at its core the belief that no man should worship another, only God. That The Way Back is not only a system of belief but should reveal through direct experience awareness of higher spirituality and communication with spiritual guides. That every human has the potential of a connection with the Spiritual Hierarchy who are themselves servants of God.

9. That all people matter and are to be respected and that all souls are created from love. We are one.

Chapter 2: Practice

The Way Back respects your right to choose what you want to believe in and they recognise and value that above all your personal experience is paramount because spirituality and the pursuit of truth is primarily concerned with experience and has little to do with belief.

What is described below is how those who founded The Way Back practice daily and is the actual guidance that the teachers of The Way Back give to their initiated students.

- Above all have God in your heart.

- Understand the teachings of the Six Virtues and practice them in your daily life, so that they can be freely expressed within your mind, heart and soul:

    - Be humble

    - Be grateful

    - Be respectful

    - Be non-judgemental

    - Be compassionate

    - Be unconditional in your love

- Acknowledge the existence of the Spiritual Hierarchy and have the intention to be receptive to guidance from your spiritual guide, conscience and soul, demonstrating trust in their guidance.

- Learn about share and reflect upon the teachings of The Way Back.

- For those who are already initiated, feel free to practice communication with your spiritual guide, through prayer, dowsing and other means.

- Practice daily meditation:

  - If a spiritual master is present then aspire to be initiated into light and sound meditation to attain enlightenment.

  - If a spiritual master is not present then practice meditation on stillness, as this is the bedrock of all spiritual development.

- Practice daily the sending of love to: yourself, the planet, your spiritual guide, the Spiritual Hierarchy and to God.

- Abstain from the taking of drugs, hallucinogenic and or medicinal plants. This includes cannabis, ayahuasca, peyote, DMT and so forth.

- Moderate or avoid the consumption of alcohol and smoking.

- Aspire to a vegetarian or vegan diet.

- Demonstrate the principle of unconditional love via the Six Virtues in daily life towards yourself, all sentient beings on Earth including animals, to the Spiritual Hierarchy and ultimately towards God.

Chapter 3: Ethos

- This journey is about service to others, not service to self. It is a journey of love, not of the ego.

- There are many purported groups of *"light and sound meditation"* but there is only one spiritual light and sound energy since there is only one source. Teachers of The Way Back are happy to support anyone from any group who demonstrates a genuine desire to progress on their spiritual journey and to embrace the virtues and values of the Spiritual Hierarchy.

- Although guidelines and advice are given to help you progress spiritually, you are respected and empowered to be self-reliant. The Way Back is not a religion or belief system, it is revelatory spiritual practice.

- The Way Back does not belong to an individual, it belongs to the Spiritual Hierarchy.

- The ascended masters of the Spiritual Hierarchy work together in harmony and clarity, putting ego aside and are aligned with love. They share a single desire to help mankind. They say "*we are one*" and are in service to God.

Postface

This concise book provides an introduction and guidance on the Six Virtues to help you on your soul and spiritual journeys, as well as in everyday life. The practical advice given enables you to more fully integrate with the different parts of what really makes you *"you"*.

I am aware that this book introduces many terms and concepts such as initiation, Spiritual Hierarchy, chakras, ego, channelling, karma, God, the Source, meditation, stillness, enlightenment and so on and that these may have sparked your interest, raised questions or even challenged you.

There is not the space in this book to fully explain these things but in-depth explanations, thorough contexts and more importantly practical guidance are available in the soon to be released book *"The Way Back to TRUTH"*, which fully explores these and many other related topics, ultimately revealing how you can find your way back to TRUTH.

With peace and love.

Mark.

Printed in Great Britain
by Amazon